CH

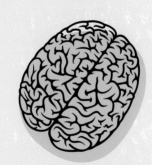

ASTROLOGICAL SIGNS

Facts, Trivia, and Quizzes

Elsie Olson

Lerner Publications ◆ Minneapolis

Lerner Publications Company
A division of Lerner Publishing Group, Inc.
241 First Avenue North
Minneapolis, MN 55401 USA

For reading levels and more information, look up this title at www.lernerbooks.com.

Main body text set in Avenir LT Pro
Typeface provided by Linotype

Library of Congress Cataloging-in-Publication Data

Names: Olson, Elsie, 1986- author.
Title: Astrological signs : facts, trivia, and quizzes / by Elsie Olson.
Description: Minneapolis : Lerner Publications, 2017. | Series: Mind games | Includes bibliographical
    references and index.
Identifiers: LCCN 2016048902 (print) | LCCN 2017004326 (ebook) | ISBN 9781512434156 (lb : alk.
    paper) | ISBN 9781512449389 (eb pdf)
Subjects: LCSH: Horoscopes—Juvenile literature.
Classification: LCC BF1728.A2 O47 2017 (print) | LCC BF1728.A2 (ebook) | DDC 133.5/4—dc23

LC record available at https://lccn.loc.gov/2016048902

Manufactured in the United States of America
1-42051-23921-1/31/2017

CONTENTS

IT'S A SIGN

It's Saturday afternoon, and you're reading your favorite magazine. You flip to the **horoscopes** to read about your sign this month. Your horoscope reads, "A stranger will become a new friend." Who could it be? On Friday, a new student told you she liked your backpack. You decide to invite the new student to eat lunch with you on Monday. This is the power of astrology!

capricorn

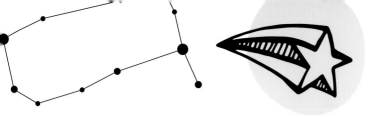

ASTROLOGY AT WORK

Astrology is a way of using movements of the sun, moon, and stars to understand the world. It has been around since ancient times. Astrology includes horoscopes. Horoscopes are based on twelve signs that relate to a person's birth date.

Astrology is not a science, but many people find it useful. It can help people think about everyday events in new ways.

Chapter 1

ANCIENT ASTROLOGY

People have studied astrology for thousands of years. The horoscopes you see most often today have their roots in ancient Babylon. It is part of what is now Iraq.

Babylonians began developing astrology as early as 3,000 BCE. They noticed that the sun and moon followed a path through twelve different **constellations**. These became the twelve constellations of the **zodiac**. In the present day, most astrologers use the zodiac as a way to help people understand themselves.

Which Element Are You?

Ancient Greeks believed people were associated with one of four elements: earth, air, fire, and water. Take the quiz below. Tally your points on a separate sheet of paper. Find out which element best fits your personality!

1. **Your best friend would say you are:**
   - *A.* **loyal** and dependable
   - *B.* the life of the party
   - *C.* a great listener
   - *D.* a problem-solver

2. **It's finally Saturday! How do you spend your free afternoon?**
   - *A.* working in your family's garden
   - *B.* rock climbing or mountain biking
   - *C.* visiting an art museum
   - *D.* hanging out with a group of friends

3. **Your school is putting on a musical. How do you participate?**
   - *A.* You help build the set. You like making things.
   - *B.* You choose the spotlight. You're the star!
   - *C.* You work on costume design. You know how to make the actors look good.
   - *D.* You become stage manager. You love working with people and organizing things.

4. **When it comes to chores, you:**
   - *A.* get to work right away and don't quit until they are done
   - *B.* put them off and then get your friends to help you
   - *C.* wait until you're in the right mood, then you get to work
   - *D.* check your planner, make a list, and do things **efficiently**

5. **You just won a dream vacation anywhere in the world! Where do you go?**
   - *A.* a cabin in the woods, where you can curl up with a book
   - *B.* a snowy mountain, where you can ski
   - *C.* a sunny beach, where you can take a swim
   - *D.* a big city with lots of things to do

ANSWERS:

Mostly As:
Down to Earth! You are a nature lover who enjoys life's comforts. Your friends can always count on you.

Mostly Bs:
You're on fire! You are adventurous and love attention. Your friends always have tons of fun with you.

Mostly Cs:
Water is your element. You are artistic and emotional. You can usually guess what your friends are feeling.

Mostly Ds:
Air all the way! You are social and a great organizer. You always look for ways to make the world a better place.

Chapter 2

WHAT'S YOUR SIGN?

Has anyone ever asked you, "What's your sign?" If so, they were probably asking your sun sign. This is the constellation the sun was in on the day you were born.

SYMBOLS AND SIGNS

Just like in ancient times, the zodiac is made up of twelve constellations. By figuring out your sun sign, astrologers claim they can tell you about your personality. Members of each sign are said to have certain **traits** in common. Each sun sign relates to one of the four elements but has its own zodiac symbol.

ophiuchus

It's True!

There are actually thirteen constellations in the zodiac. Ophiuchus, the serpent bearer, falls between Scorpio and Sagittarius. While the new sign was big news in 2011, astronomers have known about it for thousands of years. Despite this, most astrologers have continued to use the standard twelve-sign zodiac.

The 12 Signs of the Zodiac

Aries (The Ram)

Dates: March 21–April 19

Element: fire

Aries are known for being strong leaders. They think positively and are competitive. Rams are also famous for their bad tempers.

Famous Aries: Austin Mahone, Lady Gaga, Skai Jackson

Taurus (The Bull)

Dates: April 20–May 20

Element: earth

Taureans are known for being patient and **determined**. Others often rely on them. Taureans can be **stubborn** and often dislike change.

Famous Taureans: George Lucas, Robert Pattinson, William Shakespeare

Gemini (The Twins)

Dates: May 21–June 21

Element: air

Geminis are said to be smart and social. The twins are also known for mood swings. It can seem as though they have multiple personalities.

Famous Geminis: Angelina Jolie, Prince, Venus Williams

Cancer (The Crab)

Dates: June 22–July 22

Element: water

Cancers are known for being gentle and kind. They are also secretive and can hold a **grudge**.

Famous Cancers: Ariana Grande, Michael Phelps, Selena Gomez

Leo (The Lion)

Dates: July 23–August 22

Element: fire

Leos love being the center of attention. They are also loyal and natural leaders. Some can be seen as bossy.

Famous Leos: Barack Obama, Jennifer Lawrence, Joe Jonas

Virgo (The Virgin)

Dates: August 23–September 22

Element: earth

Hardworking Virgos are best known for being organized. They have a lot of energy. Some can be picky and try too hard to make everything perfect.

Famous Virgos: Blake Lively, Jimmy Fallon, Zendaya Coleman

It's True!

The astrological year begins on March 21, in the sign of Aries.

Libra (The Scales)

Dates: September 23–October 22

Element: air

Libras seek fairness and balance. However, they can also argue a lot. Some have trouble making decisions.

Famous Libras: Bruno Mars, Kim Kardashian, Maddie Ziegler

Scorpio (The Scorpion)

Dates: October 23–November 21

Element: water

Scorpios are strong-minded. They are known for their charming personalities. They can also have bad tempers and hold grudges.

Famous Scorpios: Caitlyn Jenner, Drake, Katy Perry

Sagittarius (The Archer)

Dates: November 22–December 21

Element: fire

Sagittarians love to travel. They think positively and take risks. They can also be outspoken.

Famous Sagittarians: Jake T. Austin, Miley Cyrus, Taylor Swift

Capricorn (The Goat)

Dates: December 22–January 19

Element: earth

Capricorns are known for their common sense. They are often quiet and serious.

Famous Capricorns: Kate Middleton, Liam Hemsworth, Zayn Malik

Aquarius (The Water Bearer)

Dates: January 20–February 18

Element: air

Aquarians are known for being smart and friendly. They can also be unpredictable and hard to get to know.

Famous Aquarians: Ellen DeGeneres, Harry Styles, Justin Timberlake

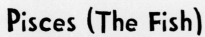

Pisces (The Fish)

Dates: February 19–March 20

Element: water

Pisces are known for their imaginations. They are also emotional. They can be easily influenced by peer pressure.

Famous Pisces: Albert Einstein, Justin Bieber, Rihanna

Do You Match Your Sun Sign?

Answer the questions and follow the arrows. Find out if your true personality matches your sun sign!

You're getting ready for the big hockey game. Are you:

the team captain?

a team player?

coming up with a new cheer to yell from the stands?

You won an award for your most recent film. What did you win?

Best Actor

Best Director

pick a pattern

pick an image

Leo!

You love performing, and you're fun to be around. But you're better at leading than following directions.

Scorpio!

You're charming and always give your best. But others better watch out when things don't go your way!

Aries!

You're a natural leader. But you sometimes get bored easily.

Capricorn!

You are wise and organized. You can become frustrated when others don't pick things up as quickly as you.

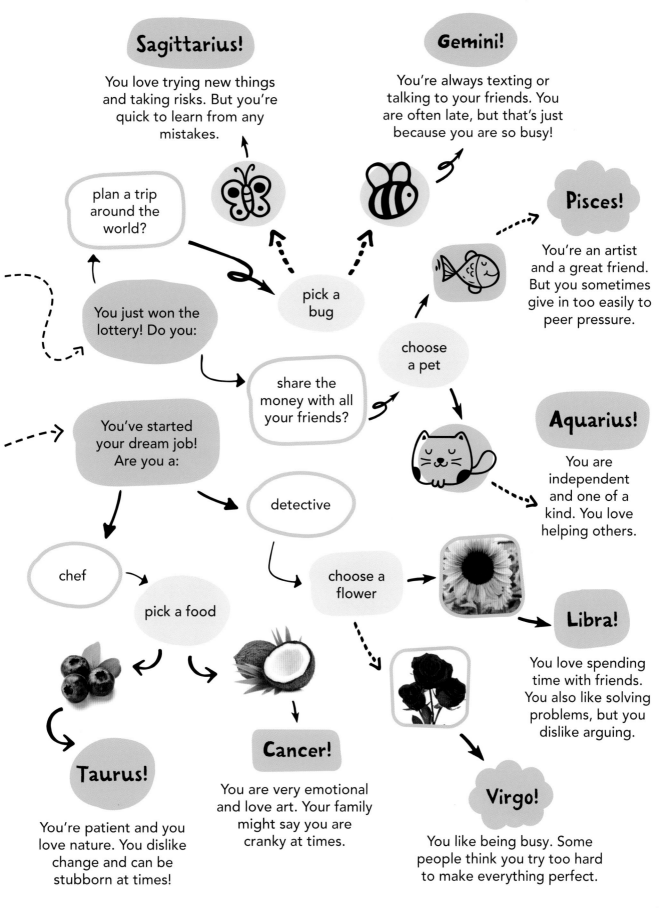

Sagittarius!

You love trying new things and taking risks. But you're quick to learn from any mistakes.

Gemini!

You're always texting or talking to your friends. You are often late, but that's just because you are so busy!

plan a trip around the world?

Pisces!

You're an artist and a great friend. But you sometimes give in too easily to peer pressure.

pick a bug

You just won the lottery! Do you:

choose a pet

share the money with all your friends?

Aquarius!

You are independent and one of a kind. You love helping others.

You've started your dream job! Are you a:

detective

chef

choose a flower

pick a food

Libra!

You love spending time with friends. You also like solving problems, but you dislike arguing.

Cancer!

You are very emotional and love art. Your family might say you are cranky at times.

Taurus!

You're patient and you love nature. You dislike change and can be stubborn at times!

Virgo!

You like being busy. Some people think you try too hard to make everything perfect.

Chapter 3
SIGNS AND SYMBOLS

In addition to the sun, modern astrologers study the location of the moon, stars, and planets at the time a person was born. From these locations, they create very detailed horoscopes called natal charts and assign rising signs and moon signs. Astrologers say these help them learn more about a person.

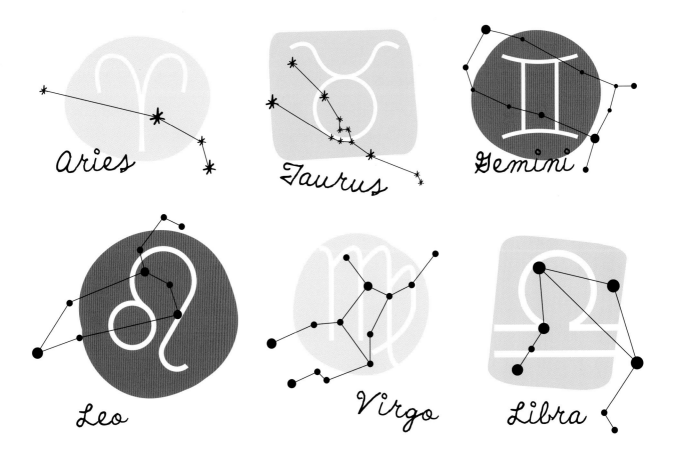

Aries

Taurus

Gemini

Leo

Virgo

Libra

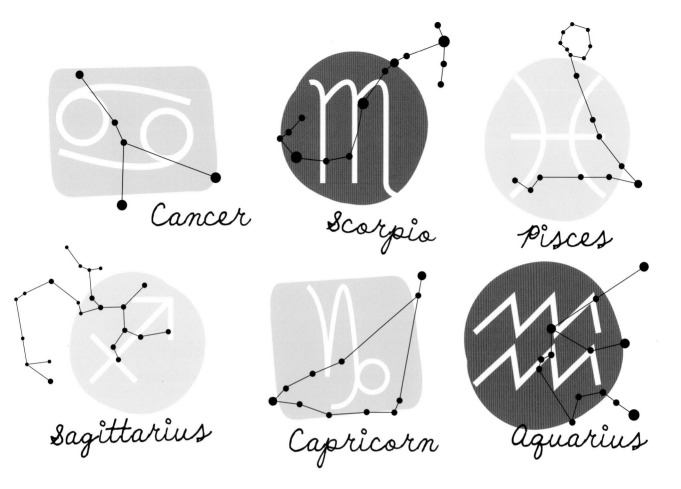

Cancer

Scorpio

Pisces

Sagittarius

Capricorn

Aquarius

RISING SIGNS

A person's rising sign depends on the time of day they were born. Astrologers believe your rising sign reflects the version of yourself that you show to the outside world. This is like wearing a mask.

What if you were born right at sunrise? Then your rising sign and sun signs are the same! That means you are like a super version of your sign, and you may show very strong **characteristics** of that sign.

MOON SIGNS

Your moon sign also relates to the time of day you were born. It depends on the moon's location during your time of birth. Moon signs help explain your feelings and moods. This is the part of yourself that only you know.

Many astrologers also look at the different stages of the moon. The moon moves through the twelve signs every two days. Some astrologers use these movements to help come up with the daily horoscopes you might see in a newspaper or online.

MOON CYCLES

Waxing Quarter Moon

Waxing Gibbous Moon

Young Moon

Full Moon

New Moon

Waning Gibbous Moon

Old Moon

Waning Quarter Moon

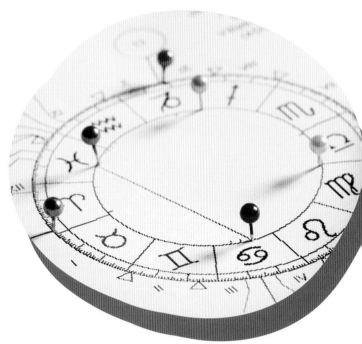

NATAL CHARTS

Professional astrologers consider many things to create natal charts. They look at sun signs, rising signs, and moon signs as well as the movement of the planets. They even consider the angles between different planets at certain times! Astrologers use these charts to describe a person's personality and to make **predictions** about trends in that person's life.

Gemini

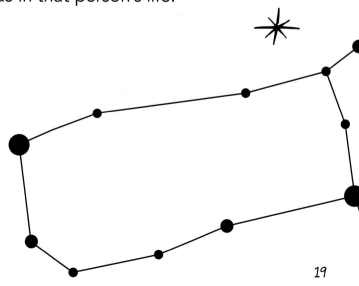

Chapter 4

THE YEAR OF YOU!

You may be most familiar with Western astrology's twelve signs of the zodiac. But Chinese astrology is very popular around the world. Its beliefs are shared in Korea, Japan, Vietnam, and other Asian countries. Unlike Western astrology, which focuses on birth date, Chinese astrology focuses on birth year.

ANNUAL ANIMALS

The Chinese zodiac has twelve animal signs. Each birth year is represented by an animal. People born in that year are said to have the traits of that animal. For example, 2006 is the year of the dog. People born in that year are said to be loyal, kind, and good listeners.

However, people born in the year of the dog better look out for 2018! That is also the year of the dog. And it's believed that when your zodiac year comes around again, you will have a year of bad luck.

The 12 Zodiac Animals

Rat

Years: 1996, 2008, 2020

Characteristics: lively, spirited, witty

Ox

Years: 1985, 1997, 2009

Characteristics: hardworking, honest, **persistent**

Tiger

Years: 1986, 1998, 2010

Characteristics: adventurous, brave, independent

Rabbit

Years: 1987, 1999, 2011

Characteristics: clever, gentle, patient

Dragon

Years: 1988, 2000, 2012

Characteristics: ambitious, enthusiastic, intelligent

Snake

Years: 1989, 2001, 2013

Characteristics: courageous, lively, wise

Sheep

Years: 1991, 2003, 2015

Characteristics: creative, honest, thoughtful

Horse

Years: 1990, 2002, 2014

Characteristics: energetic, kind, positive

It's True!

The date of the Chinese New Year changes every year, but it always falls between January 21 and February 20.

Monkey

Years: 1992, 2004, 2016

Characteristics: adventurous, **compassionate**, intelligent

Rooster

Years: 1993, 2005, 2017

Characteristics: hardworking, honest, talented

Dog

Years: 1994, 2006, 2018

Characteristics: honest, kind, loyal

Pig

Years: 1995, 2007, 2019

Characteristics: compassionate, easygoing, responsible

Find Your Animal!

Chinese astrology divides the twelve animals into four groups called trines. The animals in each trine share traits. Take the quiz below. Tally your points on a separate sheet of paper. Find out if your personality matches your birth year animal!

1. Which pizza toppings are your favorite?

A. pepperoni *(4 points)*

B. just cheese *(3 points)*

C. pineapple and Canadian bacon *(1 point)*

D. anchovies *(2 points)*

2. Which is worse?

A. cutting in line *(1 point)*

B. lying to a friend *(2 points)*

3. Choose your favorite treat.

A. red velvet cupcake *(1 point)*

B. chocolate chip cookie *(4 points)*

C. ice cream sundae *(2 points)*

D. chocolate cake *(3 points)*

4. I always do my homework right away.

A. true *(2 points)*

B. false *(1 point)*

5. Choose an after-school activity.

A. Spanish club *(2 points)*

B. school play *(1 point)*

C. chess club *(4 points)*

D. student council *(3 points)*

6. What is the most important quality in a best friend?

A. She is always there for me. *(2 points)*

B. He is lots of fun! *(1 point)*

6–9 points: First Trine! You're a rat, dragon, or monkey. You're smart and confident. Your classmates tend to like you and follow your lead.

10–12 points: Second Trine! You're a tiger, horse, or dog. You are a great friend, and you are always ready to help others.

13–15 points: Third Trine! You're an ox, snake, or rooster. You're loyal, enthusiastic, and an excellent planner.

16–18 points: Fourth Trine! You're a rabbit, pig, or sheep. You are a good student and a great listener. You always think things through.

Now that you know your trine, find out if it matches your birth year by looking on pages 22–24. Remember, if you were born in January or February, you might need to have an adult help you look up when the Chinese New Year began the year you were born.

Chapter 5

ASTROLOGY: FACT, FICTION, OR FUN?

Whether astrology is true or not, it is a cool way to learn more about yourself. Astrology encourages you to explore a new way of thinking. It gives you the chance to look at your life from a different point of view. You decide whether you think astrology is fact or fiction. Either way, you will have fun!

taurus

EXPLORE MORE!

There are many ways besides astrology to understand yourself. People also use dreams, personality quizzes, and more to learn about themselves. Explore different ways to learn more about what makes you *you*!

aquarius

Make Your Own Natal Chart!

Natal charts made by astrologers can be very detailed. But you can make a simple chart that combines everything you learned about yourself in this book!

Materials:

- 2 sheets paper
- pencil
- colored pencils, markers, stickers, and other art supplies

Step 1: Make three columns on a sheet of paper. Label one "Eastern Astrology," one "Western Astrology," and the other "Quiz Results."

Step 2: Look on pages 10–13 of this book to find your sun sign. Make a list of the characteristics of your sun sign under "Western Astrology."

Step 3: Look on pages 22–24 to find your birth year animal. Make a list of that animal's characteristics under "Eastern Astrology."

Step 4: Now look at the results of the quizzes you took on pages 7, 14–15, and 25. Write those characteristics in the "My Astrology" column. Do any of the characteristics overlap? Put a star next to any words that appear in all three columns.

Step 5: Draw a big circle on another sheet of paper. Draw a smaller circle in the center of the larger one. Then divide the larger circle into three equal parts, similar to pie slices.

Step 6: Copy the words from your first sheet of paper into the large circle. Write the Eastern words in one part, the Western words in another, and the quiz results in the third part. Write the words you starred in the smaller circle. This is your natal chart! Decorate it however you like. Then, you can use the words on your birth chart to write your own horoscope!

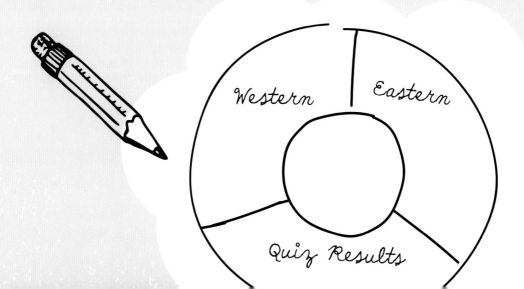

GLOSSARY

characteristics: typical features or qualities

compassionate: feeling or showing sympathy for someone who is sick or hurting

constellations: groups of stars that form shapes and have been given names

determined: having strong intent to do something

efficiently: performing or functioning in a way that wastes little time or energy

grudge: a strong feeling of anger toward someone that lasts a long time

horoscopes: advice and predictions about the future based on the positions of the stars and planets at the time of a person's birth

loyal: having or showing full and continual support for someone or something

persistent: continuing to do something or try to do something despite difficulty or obstacles

predictions: statements about what will happen in the future

stubborn: being set in your ways and not willing to give in or change

traits: qualities or characteristics

zodiac: an imaginary circle in the sky that is divided into twelve parts. The sun, moon, and planets travel through the zodiac.

FURTHER INFORMATION

Astrology

http://kids.britannica.com/comptons/article-9272987/astrology

Learn about the history of astrology from ancient times through today.

Chinese Horoscopes

http://kids.nationalgeographic.com/explore/chinese-horoscopes

Find out your birth year's animal and how it impacts your personality!

Morgan, Emily. *Next Time You See the Moon.* Arlington, VA: NSTA Kids, 2014.

Discover more about the moon's phases and how scientists can predict its cycles.

Rey, H.A. *Find the Constellations.* Boston, MA: Houghton Mifflin Harcourt, 2016.

Learn about the stars and the constellations of the zodiac.

INDEX

Photo Acknowledgments

The images in this book are used with the permission of: Design elements and doodles © alexutemov/Shutterstock.com, Fears/Shutterstock.com, mhatzapa/Shutterstock.com, Mighty Media, Inc., Miraga Niftali/Shutterstock.com, Mjosedesign/Shutterstock.com, Morphart Creation/Shutterstock.com, Nikolaeva/Shutterstock.com, Rolau Elena/Shutterstock.com, Tond Van Graphcraft/Shutterstock.com, tristan tan/Shutterstock.com, and Vector Tradition/Shutterstock.com; © Morphart Creation/Shutterstock.com, pp. 1 (top), 5 (bottom), 8 (left); © STEEX/iStockphoto.com, p. 1 (bottom); © Hasan Shaheed/Shutterstock.com, p. 3; © monkeybusinessimages/iStockphoto.com, p. 4 (top); © mixetto/iStockphoto.com, pp. 4 (middle), 27 (top); © kali9/iStockphoto.com, pp. 4 (bottom), 27 (bottom); © mammamaart/iStockphoto.com, p. 5 (top); © PeopleImages/iStockphoto.com, p. 5 (middle); © golero/iStockphoto.com, p. 8 (right); © SergeyMikhaylov/iStockphoto.com, p. 9; © Awe Inspiring Images/Shutterstock.com, p. 14 (leopard print); © Geribody/iStockphoto.com, p. 14 (snakeskin); © irin-k/Shutterstock.com, p. 15 (sunflowers); © Nella/Shutterstock.com, p. 15; © Volosina/Shutterstock.com, p. 15 (coconuts); © matin/Shutterstock.com, p. 15 (blueberries); © FatCamera/iStockphoto.com, p. 19 (left); © Jovan Nikolic/Shutterstock.com, p. 19 (right); © P_Wei/iStockphoto.com, p. 20 (left); © Rawpixel.com/Shutterstock.com, p. 20 (right); © Dan Hanscom/Shutterstock.com, p. 21; © asiseeit/iStockphoto.com, p. 26; © eurobanks/Shutterstock.com, p. 28; © Darrin Henry/Shutterstock.com, p. 29; © Twin Design/Shutterstock.com, p. 31.

Front cover: © Morphart Creation/Shutterstock.com (top, left); © PeopleImages/iStockphoto.com (top, right); © STEEX/iStockphoto.com (middle); © gradyreese/iStockphoto.com (bottom, left).

Back cover: © PeopleImages/iStockphoto.com (left); © mixetto/iStockphoto.com (right).